GOSPEL SONGS FOR FINGERSTYLE GUITAR

A rich collection of 17 solo arrangements, in a variety of tunings, with standard notation, tablature, background information, and humorous asides

By Steve Baughman

string
letter
media

Publisher: David A. Lusterman
Editor: Adam Perlmutter
Managing Editor: Kevin Owens
Design and Production: Bill Evans
Production Manager: Hugh O'Connor

Cover Photograph: Joey Lusterman

ISBN 978-1-936604-33-3

This book was produced by Stringletter Media, Inc.
501 Canal Blvd., Suite J, Richmond, CA 94804
(510) 215-0010; stringletter.com

Contents

Video downloads to accompany each of the lessons in *Gospel Songs For Fingerstyle Guitar* are available for free at **store.acousticguitar.com/GSFG**. Just add the video tracks to your shopping cart and check out to get your free download.

Introduction

I once had the chance to ask the self-professed "hardline atheist" Salman Rushdie why he loved old Christian hymns so much. His answer: that tremendous human talent and spirit has been poured into creating them.

True enough. But surely that is so of all music, or at least of most music. What is it about hymns and gospel music that so engages us across philosophical lines? Surely it is not their theology, for that does not explain their wide appeal to nonbelievers. In fact, sometimes the music speaks movingly despite the seeming implausibility of the message. A group of lepers at a sanitarium in the Philippines once gathered around me and my guitar, and we sang "Whispering Hope" together.

Whispering hope, oh how welcome thy voice
Making my heart in its sorrow rejoice.

How much hope did these people have? I did not know. Perhaps they didn't either. But rejoicing happened. And this, it seems to me, is why the old hymns remain so stably in our hearts; they speak of universal human longings. Horatio Spafford wrote "It Is Well With My Soul" in 1873 after receiving news that his four daughters had been lost when the steamship *Ville du Havre* went down in the Atlantic.

When sorrows like sea billows roll
Whatever my lot, Thou hast taught me to say
It is well, it is well with my soul.

It requires no religious sentiments to make the tears well up as we encounter these words and their musical rendering. All it takes is that we be human.

The philosopher Theodor Adorno once complained that activist music "takes the horrendous and makes it somehow consumable." This does not seem to capture the experience that I describe of sacred music. The comfort, nourishment, and inspiration that the old hymns deliver are no mere matters of consumption; these songs engage us at our very core.

Now for the awkward question: This is a book of instrumental guitar arrangements of hymns. Instrumentals have no words. How then can they speak of anything, much less of our deepest longings? Well, instrumentals may not have words, but they do have associations. And the fact that you hold this book in your hands may mean that those associations are significant for you. I suspect that you may also have some of the lyrics in your head and will be singing them internally as you give these melodies a voice through your guitar. The words are always with me as I play these songs.

I grew up with hymns, and arranging them for the guitar has been a passion for me. These arrangements range from intermediate to very advanced. The slow part of "Nearer, My God, to Thee" is at the intermediate end of the spectrum; the fast part, on the other end. The slow part shows how much beauty one can create on the guitar with a combination of passion and intermediate-level picking skills.

On several of the arrangements in this book I use techniques that are not very widely employed in the fingerstyle world, like recurring downward middle-finger brushes and the pinching that mimics a flatpick feel. These elements are notated clearly, and I encourage you to pay attention to them. The feel is better when the picking hand is not just banging out notes.

By the way—and finally, despite my spiel about the richness of Christian hymns and how they speak to us—sometimes a melody, like a cigar, is just a melody. Each of the ones presented in this book stands on its own as a gorgeous piece of music with or without the text that has historically accompanied it. If all you want is to have fun with these tunes, that's okay. My hope is that this book helps you embark on a rich and rewarding journey, spiritual or otherwise.

—Steve Baughman

Notation Guide

Reading music is no different than reading a book. In both cases, you need to understand the language that you're reading; you can't read Chinese characters if you don't understand them, and you can't read music if you don't understand the written symbols behind music notation.

Guitarists use several types of notation, including standard notation, tablature, and chord grids. Standard notation is the main notation system common to all instruments and styles in Western music. Knowing standard notation will allow you to share and play music with almost any other instrument. Tablature is a notation system exclusively for stringed instruments with frets—like guitar and mandolin—that shows you what strings and frets to play at any given moment. Chord grids use a graphic representation of the fretboard to show chord shapes for fretted stringed instruments. Here's a primer on how to read these types of notation.

Standard Notation

Standard notation is written on a five-line staff. Notes are written in alphabetical order from A to G. Every time you pass a G note, the sequence of notes repeats—starting with A.

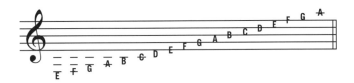

The duration of a note is determined by three things: the note head, stem, and flag. A whole note (o) equals four beats. A half note (♩) is half of that: two beats. A quarter note (♩) equals one beat, an eighth note (♪) equals half of one beat, and a 16th note (♬) is a quarter beat (there are four 16th notes per beat).

The fraction (4/4, 3/4, 6/8, etc.) or ¢ character shown at the beginning of a piece of music denotes the time signature. The top number tells you how many beats are in each measure, and the bottom number indicates the rhythmic value of each beat (4 equals a quarter note, 8 equals an eighth note, 16 equals a 16th note, and 2 equals a half note).

The most common time signature is 4/4, which signifies four quarter notes per measure and is sometimes designated with the symbol ¢ (for common time). The symbol ¢ stands for cut time (2/2). Most songs are either in 4/4 or 3/4.

Tablature

In tablature, the six horizontal lines represent the six strings of the guitar, with the first string on the top and sixth on the bottom. The numbers refer to fret numbers on a given string.

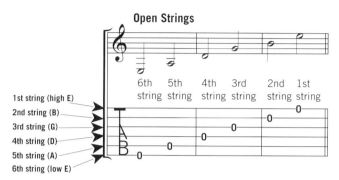

The notation and tablature in this book are designed to be used in tandem—refer to the notation to get the rhythmic information and note durations, and refer to the tablature to get the exact locations of the notes on the guitar fingerboard.

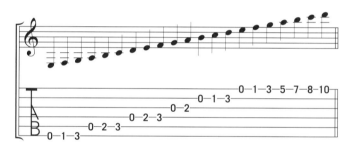

Fingerings

Fingerings are indicated with small numbers and letters in the notation. Fretting-hand fingering is indicated with 1 for the index finger, 2 middle, 3 the ring, 4 the pinky, and *T* the thumb. Picking-hand fingering is indicated by *i* for the index finger, *m* the middle, *a* the ring, *c* the pinky, and *p* the thumb. Circled numbers indicate the string the note is played on. Remember that the fingerings indicated are only suggestions; if you find a different way that works better for you, use it.

Strumming and Picking

In music played with a flatpick, downstrokes (toward the floor) and upstrokes (toward the ceiling) are shown as follows. Slashes in the notation and tablature indicate a strum through the previously played chord.

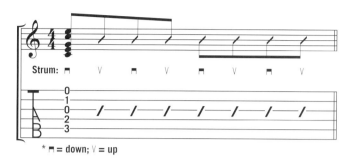

In music played with the pick-hand fingers, *split stems* are often used to highlight the division between thumb and fingers. With split stems, notes played by the thumb have stems pointing down, while notes played by the fingers have stems pointing up. If split stems are not used, pick-hand fingerings are usually present. Here is the same fingerpicking pattern shown with and without split stems.

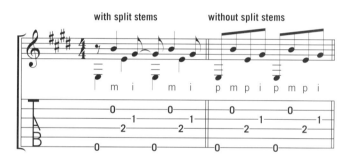

Chord Diagrams

Chord diagrams show where the fingers go on the fingerboard. Frets are shown horizontally. The thick top line represents the nut. A fret number to the right of a diagram indicates a chord played higher up the neck (in this case the top horizontal line is thin). Strings are shown as vertical lines. The line on the far left represents the sixth (lowest) string, and the line on the far right represents the first (highest) string. Dots show where the fingers go, and thick horizontal lines indicate barres. Numbers above the diagram are left-hand finger numbers, as used in standard notation.

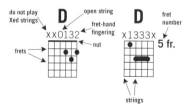

Again, the fingerings are only suggestions. An *X* indicates a string that should be muted or not played; 0 indicates an open string.

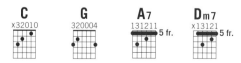

Capos

If a capo is used, a Roman numeral indicates the fret where the capo should be placed. The standard notation and tablature is written as if the capo were the nut of the guitar. For instance, a tune capoed anywhere up the neck and played using key-of-G chord shapes and fingerings will be written in the key of G. Likewise, open strings held down by the capo are written as open strings.

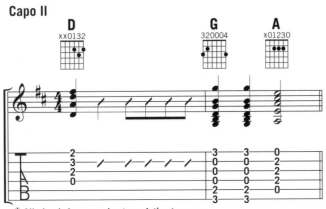

* All chord shapes and notes relative to capo

Tunings

Alternate guitar tunings are given from the lowest (sixth) string to the highest (first) string. For instance, D A D G B E indicates standard tuning with the bottom string dropped to D. Standard notation for songs in alternate tunings always reflects the actual pitches of the notes. Arrows underneath tuning notes indicate strings that are altered from standard tuning and whether they are tuned up or down.

Tuning: D A D G B E

Vocal Tunes

Vocal tunes are sometimes written with a fully tabbed-out introduction and a vocal melody with chord diagrams for the rest of the piece. The tab intro is usually your indication of which strum or fingerpicking pattern to use in the rest of the piece. The melody with lyrics underneath is the melody sung by the vocalist. Occasionally, smaller notes are written with the melody to indicate other instruments or the harmony part sung by another vocalist. These are not to be confused with cue notes, which are small notes that indicate melodies that vary when a section is repeated. Listen to a recording of the piece to get a feel for the guitar accompaniment and to hear the singing if you aren't skilled at reading vocal melodies.

Articulations

There are a number of ways you can articulate a note on the guitar. Notes connected with slurs (not to be confused with ties) in the tablature or standard notation are articulated with either a hammer-on, pull-off, or slide. Lower notes slurred to higher notes are played as hammer-ons; higher notes slurred to lower notes are played as pull-offs.

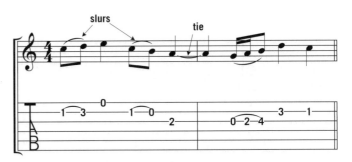

Slides are represented with a dash, and an S is included above the tab. A dash preceding a note represents a slide into the note from an indefinite point in the direction of the slide; a dash following a note indicates a slide off of the note to an indefinite point in the direction of the slide. For two slurred notes connected with a slide, you should pick the first note and then slide into the second.

Bends are represented with upward curves, as shown in the next example. Most bends have a specific destination pitch—the number above the bend symbol shows how much the bend raises the string's pitch: ¼ for a slight bend, ½ for a half step, 1 for a whole step.

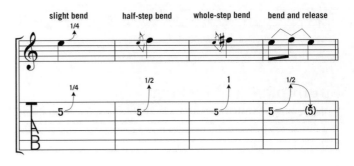

Grace notes are represented by small notes with a dash through the stem in standard notation and with small numbers in the tab. A grace note is a very quick ornament leading into a note, most commonly executed as a hammer-on, pull-off, or slide. In the first example below, pluck the note at the fifth fret on the beat, then quickly hammer onto the seventh fret. The second example is executed as a quick pull-off from the second fret to the open string. In the third example, both notes at the fifth fret are played simultaneously (even though it appears that the fifth fret, fourth string, is to be played by itself), then the seventh fret, fourth string, is quickly hammered.

Harmonics

Harmonics are represented by diamond-shaped notes in the standard notation and a small dot next to the tablature numbers. Natural harmonics are indicated with the text "Harmonics" or "Harm." above the tablature. Harmonics articulated with the right hand (often called artificial harmonics) include the text "R.H. Harmonics" or "R.H. Harm." above the tab. Right-hand harmonics are executed by lightly touching the harmonic node (usually 12 frets above the open string or fretted note) with the right-hand index finger and plucking the string with the thumb or ring finger or pick. For extended phrases played with right-hand harmonics, the fretted notes are shown in the tab along with instructions to touch the harmonics 12 frets above the notes.

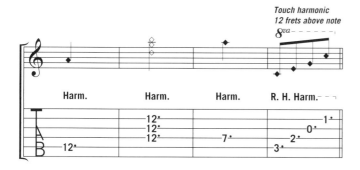

Repeats

One of the most confusing parts of a musical score can be the navigation symbols, such as repeats, *D.S. al Coda*, *D.C. al Fine*, *To Coda*, etc. Repeat symbols are placed at the beginning and end of the passage to be repeated.

You should ignore repeat symbols with the dots on the right side the first time you encounter them; when you come to a repeat symbol with dots on the left side, jump back to the previous repeat symbol facing the opposite direction (if there is no previous symbol, go to the beginning of the piece). The next time you come to the repeat symbol, ignore it and keep going unless it includes instructions such as "Repeat three times."

A section will often have a different ending after each repeat. The example below includes a first and a second ending. Play until you hit the repeat symbol, jump back to the previous repeat symbol and play until you reach the bracketed first ending, skip the measures under the bracket and jump immediately to the second ending, and then continue.

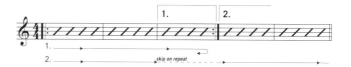

D.S. stands for *dal segno* or "from the sign." When you encounter this indication, jump immediately to the sign (𝄋). *D.S.* is usually accompanied by *al Fine* or *al Coda*. Fine indicates the end of a piece. A coda is a final passage near the end of a piece and is indicated with ⊕. *D.S. al Coda* simply tells you to jump back to the sign and continue on until you are instructed to jump to the coda, indicated with *To Coda* ⊕.

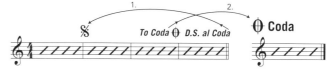

D.C. stands for *da capo* or "from the beginning." Jump to the top of the piece when you encounter this indication.

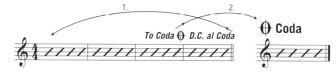

D.C. al Fine tells you to jump to the beginning of a tune and continue until you encounter the *Fine* indicating the end of the piece (ignore the *Fine* the first time through).

Down by the Riverside

I have arranged "Down by the Riverside"—a traditional song that, depending on who you ask, is about meeting Jesus or your brown-eyed girl by the river, or casting aside the instruments of war—as a straight alternating-bass piece. As you explore the arrangement, take notice of the inclusion of a very useful single-string "pinch" technique in measures 3, 8, and 11. The thumb proceeds as though on autopilot (a very important ingredient of most alternating-bass tunes), but the index finger interjects a quick pluck immediately preceding the thumb on the same string. This maneuver can be a bit tricky, but it is a great skill to have when the melody falls on a string that the thumb is about to strike. You can often get away with fudging it,

but getting it to emerge clearly and without a rhythmic glitch can provide quite a triumphant feeling!

Another useful feature of this arrangement is the bluesy G chord sound first heard in measure 29. By holding a standard G chord and fretting the third string at the third fret you get a G major chord with a blue note (B♭, the minor third) that clashes exquisitely with the major third (B, on the open second string). I find this to be a wonderful sound. Using blue notes to tweak your listeners' ears and push the boundaries between major and minor will serve you particularly well in fingerstyle arrangements of your own—guaranteed!

Energetically

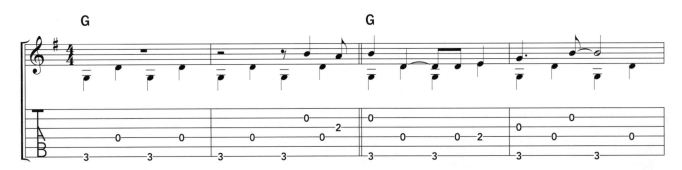

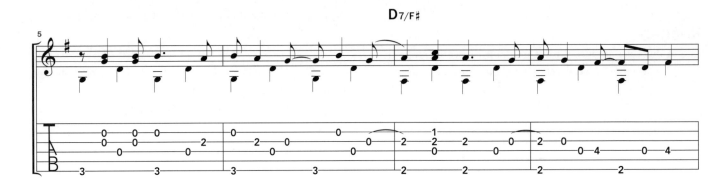

Fairest Lord Jesus

One of my earliest musical memories is hearing "Fairest Lord Jesus," a favorite piece of my grandfather's. I learned it on harmonica when I was first starting on the instrument, and I was amazed at how easy it was to play. I gave up harmonica very shortly after that, but I've stayed with the guitar and have arranged this gorgeous melody—which works really nicely in standard tuning—for solo guitar.

One of the aspects I like best about this arrangement is the use of a nice F chord in fifth position (bar 7)—a useful shape to know if you're not already acquainted with it. Play the F chord with your first finger barring strings 1–3 at fret 5 and your second finger on the sixth-fret F; grab the eighth-fret C with your fourth finger.

I also like bringing in that gorgeous A7 chord in bar 13. In technical terms, this is a secondary dominant chord, which is to say it's a V chord that resolves to a chord other than the tonic (C in the key of C major.) The A7 acts as the V of the Dm chord it precedes, giving a feeling of movement to the arrangement.

For a welcome change of texture, in the second section (bars 21–32), I play the melody with my thumb on the lower strings while adding light chordal flourishes on the upper strings. Be sure to play the melody notes more loudly than the chords. Lightly brush the chords that fall on the beats downwards with your middle finger, and use your index finger for those on the *ands* of beats. Or, if you'd like, eliminate some or all of the chords—make it your own and have fun with it.

Great Is Thy Faithfulness

lthough the lyrics to "Great Is Thy Faithfulness" make it a classic hymn of praise with an unmistakably religious message, the melody is so sweet that guitar players of any philosophical orientation should find pleasure in learning to play it. The song became widely known when Billy Graham started using it at the events he called "crusades," and it also made the rounds at Christian schools across the United States.

Your old reliable I, IV, and V chords aren't quite enough to get you through this tune, but I think this arrangement shows how easy it is to spice up your chordal vocabulary with some very simple finger movements. I am particularly fond of the B9/D# chord in measures 12 and 28, a brief secondary domi-

nant chord created through a simple move that really adds to the musical depth of the arrangement.

You may notice a little bit of fretting-hand finger crunching at times (as in measures 19 and 20), but nothing too frightening—on the whole, this arrangement should be fairly easy to deliver. As you play, you'll notice a fair amount of activity in the picking-hand thumb, which injects moving bass lines between and under melody notes. In measure 33, the arrangement kicks into a second verse with the melody shifted to a lower octave. I find it very refreshing to then return to the regular octave as the arrangement moves back to the D.S. at measure 17.

Pass Me Not, Oh Gentle Savior

Do a search for "Pass Me Not, Oh Gentle Savior," and you'll find that this piece is all over the map in terms of the many different ways in which it's been arranged. I aim to contribute to that diversity by playing it in a time-honored country-blues approach. Not only does the simple melody of "Pass Me Not" work out nicely in this setting, the arrangement is also really good training for learning to play an alternating-thumb pattern and a sweet melody simultaneously.

I'm pretty much doing alternating thumb throughout, save for a few little variations, such as the turnaround in bars 17–18, where I temporarily depart from the pattern for rhythmic effect. The goal is to keep your thumb going constantly, as if on autopilot, such that you can breathe and talk at the same time.

Country-blues guitar parts tend to revolve around open-chord shapes, and for the most part, this arrangement is no exception. But in certain spots, I opt for less common voicings: instead of doing a basic open E chord in bar 9 and elsewhere, for instance, I use a grip with my first finger on string 4, fret 2; my third finger on string 3, fret 4; and my fourth finger on string 1, fret 4.

Another thing I do is appropriate the Doc Watson "Deep River" E7 chord, like in bars 35–36, where I play the sixth-fret G# with my second finger, the eighth-fret G with my fourth finger, and the seventh-fret B with my third finger. Although the quarter-step bend on that G is essential to a bluesy flavor, remember that, above all, making sure your thumb is on autopilot is what's crucial for bringing out the melody with ease.

Rock of Ages

In 1763, the Rev. Augustus Montague Toplady wrote what would become one of the most beloved songs in gospel literature, "Rock of Ages." This beautiful, simple melody just works so well on fingerstyle guitar, and it's a real treat to play in the guitar-friendly key of A major.

One of the things I really enjoy about this arrangement is the beauty you can get out of playing single-note lines. It's a slow, emotive song, and I really enjoy taking the melody down an octave, as I do beginning in bar 12, and throwing in just a little bit of filler courtesy of the open first and second strings. This adds a little texture to the arrangement, but is totally optional.

Because the piece is so short, it begs for the sort of cascading chordal variations I play beginning in bar 25. This portion is based not on the "Rock of Ages" melody but on two very important chord shapes that I really want you to know about: the "Deep River Blues" E7 chord (also use in "Pass Me Not, Oh Gentle Savior" and other arrangements) and a fifth-position A chord—the first finger barring strings 1 and 2 at the fifth fret, second finger on the sixth-fret C♯, and the third finger on the seventh-fret A. By adding notes around these two shapes and playing around with pull-offs and other articulations, you can improvise some cascading variations—an excellent opportunity to make this gorgeous piece your own.

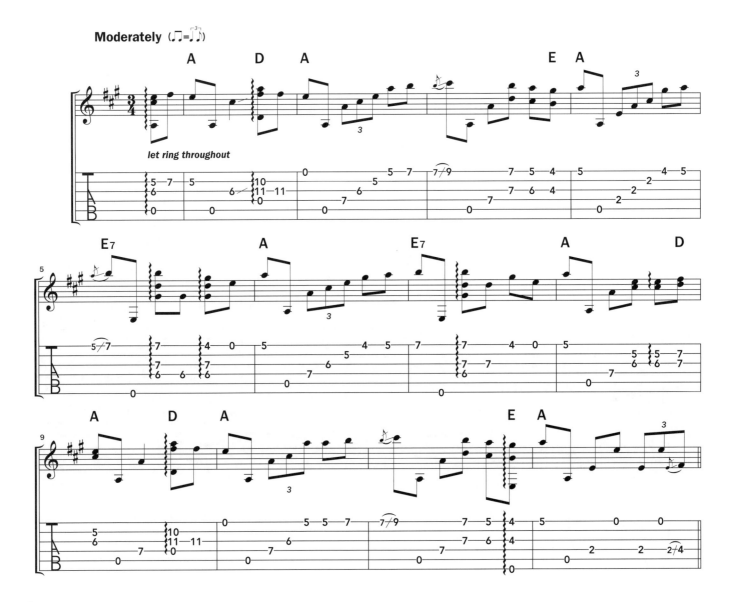

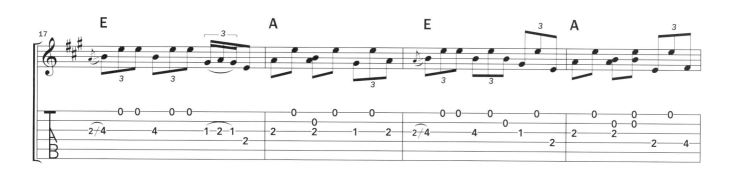

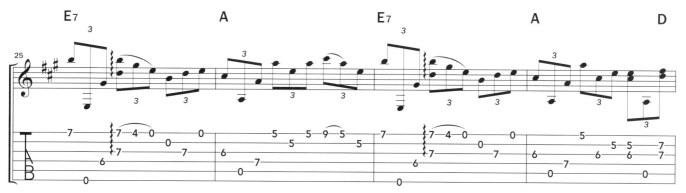

Shall We Gather at the River

ere's a good old-time gospel tune that's about as blue-grass as they get—an arrangement that works quite nicely with a thumb-led approach in the mold of "Mother" Maybelle Carter. I play it in the key of C, which gives me lots of ringing open notes.

Throughout the arrangement, you'll notice my fourth finger hanging out quite a bit at the third-fret G on string 1. I do this when I'm playing the I chord (C), the IV (F), and the V (G). I like the sound of that high fifth (as opposed to the open first string) on the C chord, and on the F chord, the G note makes for a colorful Fadd9 voicing. Overall, the high G makes for a smooth transition between the I, IV, and V, as it's common to all three chords. It also adds a bit of brightness to the arrangement.

The fretting hand has the most important role in the piece. I wear fingerpicks when I play it, but you could also do it finger-style. The basic picking pattern is shown in bar 1: thumbed bass notes squarely on beats 1 and 3, and chordal accents—a brush down with the thumb, followed by an upstroke of the index finger—on 2 and 4. Make sure that you have this pattern down before tackling the rest of the piece.

When I run through the tune a second time, starting in bar 35, I weave in single-note lines, inspired by bluegrass flatpicking. Basically, I pick the notes on the beats with my thumb, and those on the *ands* with my index finger. Again, it's really important to have the basic melody and accompaniment pattern in your blood before you can add those fills. Once you're ready to tackle these bluegrass effects, things get to be really fun.

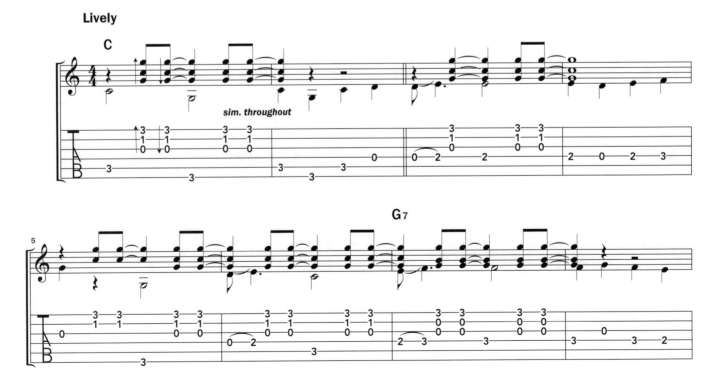

When the Roll Is Called Up Yonder

"When the Roll Is Called Up Yonder" is a song I learned from my father, as it was one of his all-time favorites. We used to sing it together when I was a little kid, before I even began playing guitar. Now I like to do the piece as a really fun alternating-thumb arrangement.

As with any piece using this approach, the key is simply to get your picking-hand thumb going and play a melody over it with your fingers. The tricky thing about this particular arrangement is that you can't get away with doing the melody in straight quarter notes. That would be nice, but the melody is quite syncopated and doesn't line up exactly with the bass notes, making things harder.

The arrangement is great practice, though, for learning how to not have your fingers be slaves to quarter notes.

Another thing the piece is good for is really impressing people—which, granted, isn't why you should be playing guitar. But sometimes it's fun to throw out a hot riff. And the chromatic lick at the end of the piece, starting in bar 67, might sound flashy, but it's not all that hard to play. The pattern is the same on each string: open string, first fret, second fret, third fret, picked in alternating strokes of the thumb and index finger. Put in the time to learn to play this passage cleanly, and it will wow people every time.

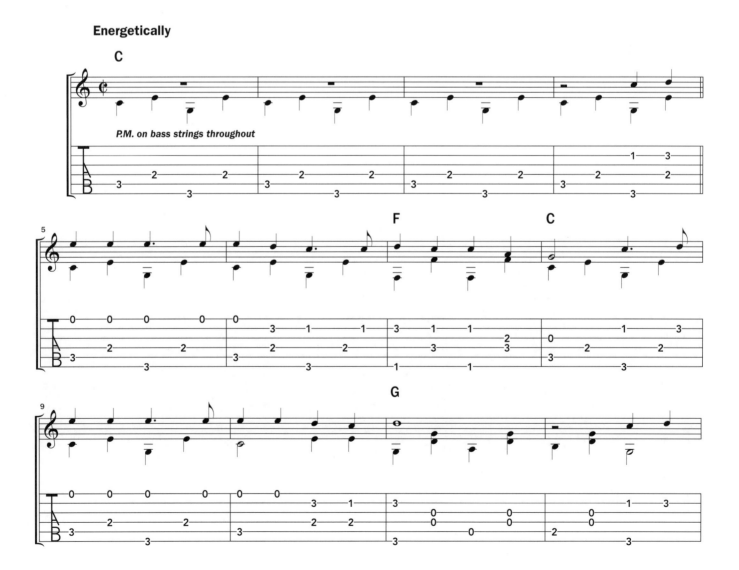

At Calvary

"At Calvary" is a great old gospel hymn, one I've sung my whole life. It's one of those rousing kinds of songs, and my recommendation is that when you play it on guitar, you try to capture the sound of a church choir singing together in that high-energy kind of way.

If you glance at the notation, you'll notice that I don't do a lot of single-string playing in this arrangement, because I'm trying to evoke the sound of voices singing together in harmony. Playing the song in open G also helps me recreate that kind of choir feel.

I brush the strings liberally with my thumb when playing the piece; since I'm in an open tuning, I don't need to worry about hitting the strings accurately, and the brushes enhance the overall feeling of the piece. Still, I do try to capture the independently moving voices of the choir, and you can see this in the bass patterns of bars 8, 16, and elsewhere.

You might have noticed that the music in bars 1–16 is essentially the same as measures 17–32, but there are lots of subtle variations between these two sections. For example, compare bar 8 to its counterpart, bar 24, and you'll see I added rolled eighth-note triplets in the latter measure. After you've learned my arrangement, be sure to apply some of your own flourishes to this spirited hymn. And remember to really make it sing.

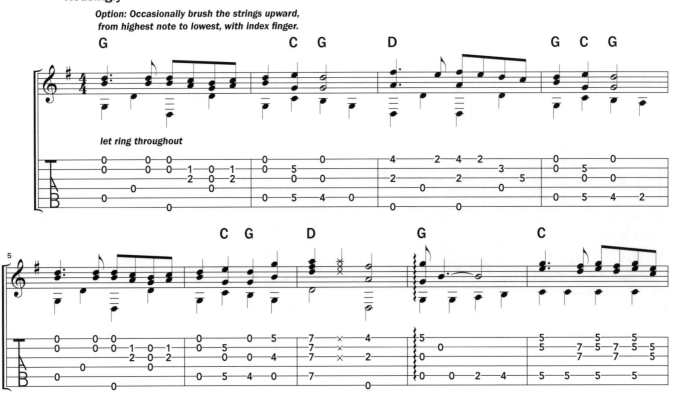

Tuning: D G D G B D

Rousingly

Option: Occasionally brush the strings upward, from highest note to lowest, with index finger.

let ring throughout

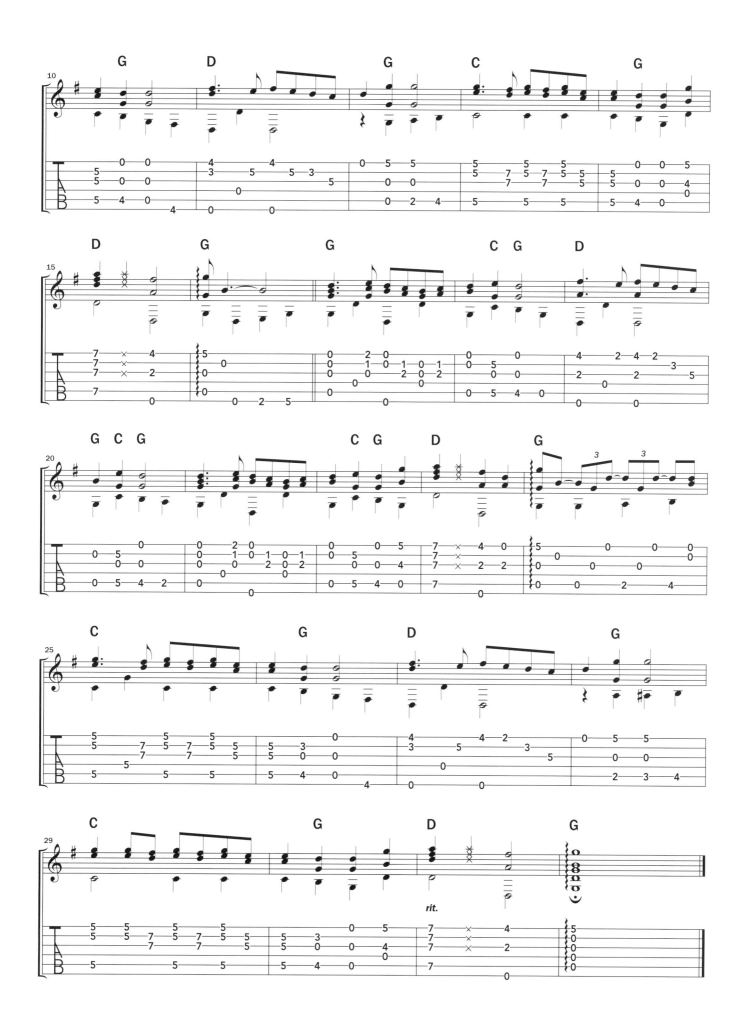

Just As I Am

This piece, which the late Rev. Billy Graham had playing at his "crusades," is one of the most famous American hymns. If you grew up in a Southern Baptist church—or any Protestant congregation for that matter—you probably know "Just As I Am" very well.

One of the techniques this arrangement uses a lot of is a style of strumming I call Lubus picking, which I learned from the late North Carolina guitarist Joe Lubus. I recommend practicing the Lubus approach by picking a bass note with your thumb, brushing a chord down on the upper strings with your middle finger, and then brushing it up with your index finger. Work on the pattern slowly, until it becomes second nature. If Lubus picking is new to you, spend some time training your picking hand to play it smoothly and effortlessly.

Pick the fingerstyle chords—which are generally indicated by arpeggio markings (squiggly vertical lines)—quickly from lowest note to highest, using your thumb, index, and middle or ring fingers. Most important, you really want the arrangement to sing, so play it as smoothly as possible. Try to capture the slow and somber feeling that the tune requires, while making every note speak.

Tuning: D G D G B D

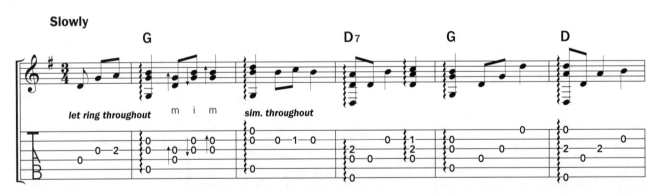

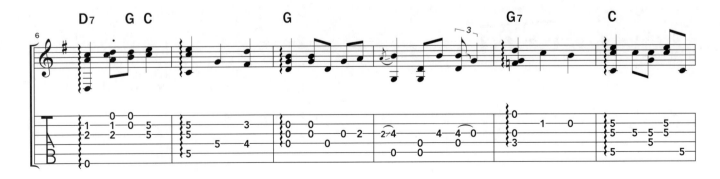

Old Rugged Cross

"Old Rugged Cross," one of the classic Southern hymns, is usually done with a high-energy choir singing at the top of its lungs, full of joy and vivaciousness and all that. But I play it in taro patch (open-G) tuning as sort of a Hawaiian slack-key guitar arrangement, mellowing it out by about 90 percent.

One of the things I like about playing this arrangement—other than I love the piece dearly—is the opportunity for a great amount of resonance. Open G is just a wonderful tuning for playing in the key of G major, with all those ringing open strings. But there are times when it's OK—and even desirable—to cut the ringing, as I do when I play fully fretted double stops in bar 3 and elsewhere, for instance. These interruptions in texture work really well if done properly and smoothly.

Another thing I like to do is drop the melody by an octave and pick it with my thumb, which I do beginning on beat 3 of bar 32. It's really fun and you can be very emotive with it. One thing to be mindful of: When doing filler strums, you really have to consider the chord. On a G chord, like in measures 33–34, you can of course hit the open strings, but for the C and A chords in bars 35 and 36, respectively, you'll want to form C- and A-chord grips. That way you don't have to worry about hitting the wrong notes on those chordal decorations.

What's most important is that every note just cries in "Old Rugged Cross." Remember to make sure that it sounds highly emotional throughout. It's not about the formula but the feeling.

Tuning: D G D G B D
Flowing

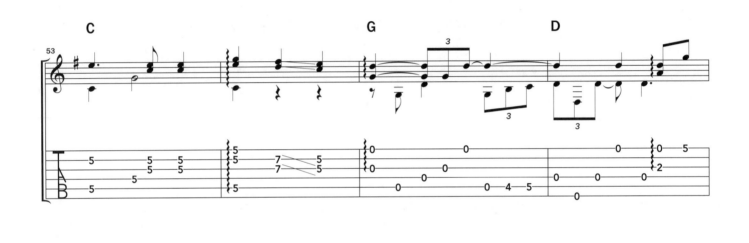

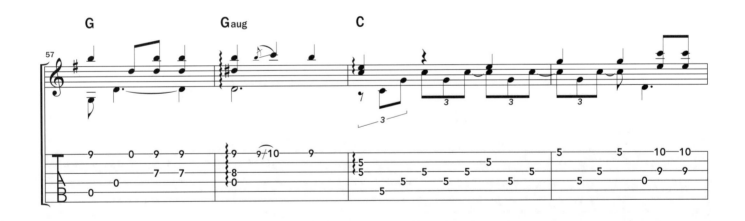

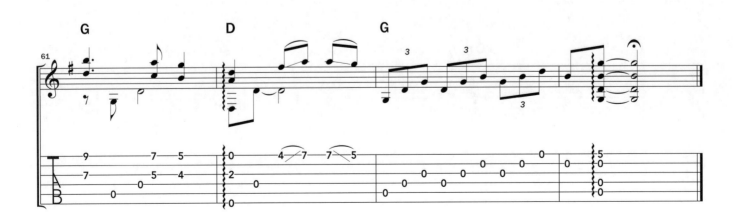

Whispering Hope

This is one of the tunes that is really near and dear to my heart. The first time I remember playing it for anybody was at a leper colony in the Philippines. I just happened to show up, and being young, I traveled everywhere with my guitar. I'm old now and still travel everywhere with my guitar. So should you.

But I digress. These folks at the leper colony all gathered around me and started singing. They knew a lot of songs but fell silent when I started playing "Whispering Hope"—that is, until the rousing chorus came along and they all joined in singing. It was one of the best moments of my musical life, and a really great reminder of how unifying music can be, taking us across classes, across borders, and across health statuses.

The song is usually done very bombastically, but I prefer to play it in more of a laidback Hawaiian style. Like I do on "Just As I Am," I'm using Lubus picking—strumming down with my thumb, down with my middle finger, and up with my index. It's very important when playing "Whispering Hope" to have that strum flow gently.

Another detail I'd like to point out is my use of an oddball chord I call "A-demented" (A7♭9) in bar 12. If you don't like the sound or feel of this chord, you could eliminate the flatted ninth (third-fret B♭) and play an A7 chord by barring strings 1–5 at the second fret and grabbing the fifth-fret G with your fourth finger on string 1. Let your ears be the guide here.

Tuning: D G D G B D

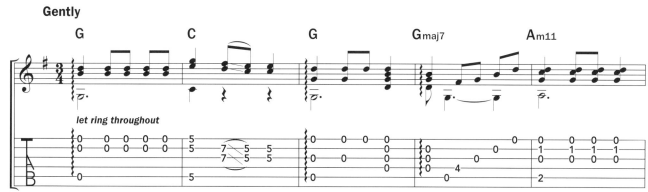

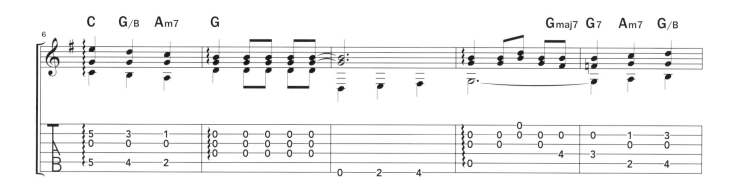

Go Tell It on the Mountain

The spiritual "Go Tell It on the Mountain" dates back to at least 1865, but it was updated and secularized in 1963 by Peter, Paul and Mary, who replaced the words "Jesus Christ is born" with "Let my people go." Fair's fair in the folk process! For us, this means a piece that we can play year round—the original lyrics make it a great Christmas tune, and the update makes it acceptable to play between the months of January and November.

I have arranged "Go Tell It on the Mountain" here as an alternating-thumb piece with a bit of a bluesy feel. Those of you with lots of experience in Travis picking may find this arrangement quite accessible, and beginning alternating-thumb players should find this to be a good piece to get started on for playing a melody while keeping your thumb on autopilot.

This arrangement instantiates a bit of good advice I got from another hymn-arranging enthusiast, the fingerstyle guitarist El McMeen: When a piece of music is short, as most hymns are,

avoid over-repetition by moving parts of your arrangement to a higher or lower octave. In this piece, the verse melody (heard first in the higher octave in measures 3–10) is played in a low octave beginning in measure 19. This section offers a chance to practice your alternating-thumb technique while playing a melody on the middle strings—a somewhat tricky but very useful skill!

As you tackle the arrangement, I recommend slightly muting the bass strings with your picking-hand palm to enhance the percussive groove of the piece. This is an important skill to have—place the heel of your picking hand gently on the bass strings and see if you can create that muting while you pick the bass strings. It's worth playing around with the angle and position of your picking hand until you can lock in that sound. You'll know you've got it right when you can keep that muted bass thumping while still allowing the treble notes to ring out.

Tuning: D A D G B D

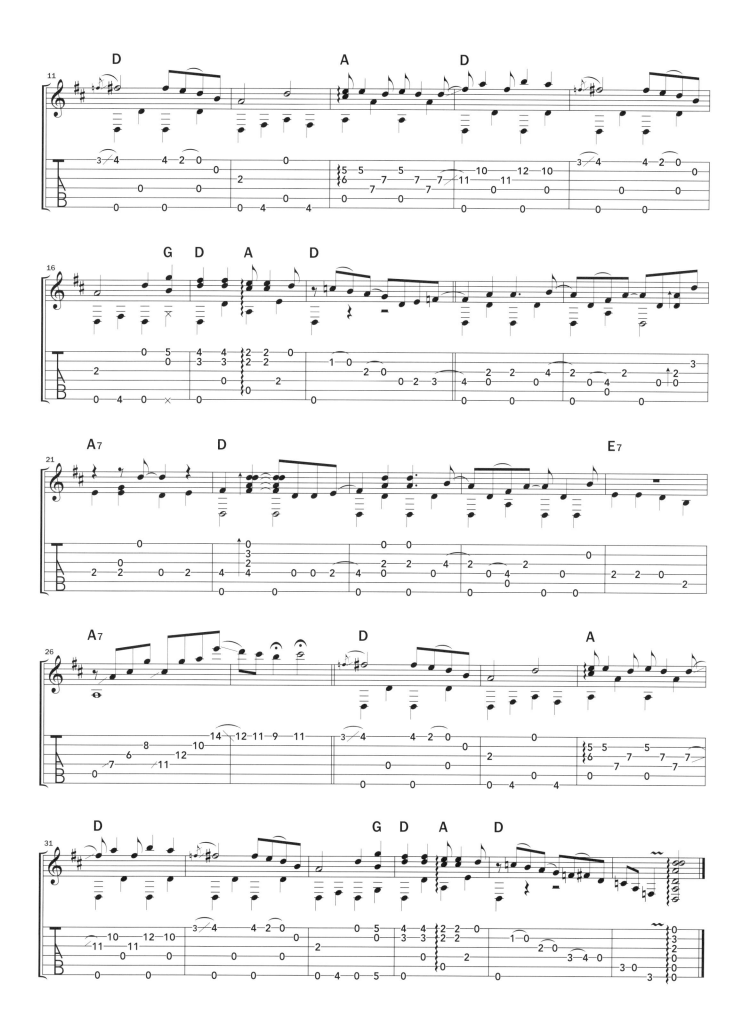

It Is Well With My Soul

This is a beautiful old hymn with a tragic background. You can Google it for the full details, but here's the story in a nutshell: The piece was written in 1873 by a big Chicago businessman, Horatio Spafford, after receiving word that his four daughters had drowned in a ship accident. So "It Is Well With My Soul" is a beautiful melody, attached to a very touching story, and it's quite satisfying to play on fingerstyle guitar in double-dropped-D tuning.

In terms of the picking hand, there's nothing unusual about the technique here. As with any piece, pick the notes on the bottom strings with your thumb and those on the higher strings with your index, middle, and ring fingers. The fretting hand's contribu-tions are also fairly straightforward, save for an awful stretch between frets 2 and 6, on beat 4 of bar 30. If this stretch is too difficult, just play the E an octave higher, on string 5, fret 7. You won't ruin the funeral if you play it in that location.

Be sure to play "It Is Well With My Soul" unhurriedly and with emotion—keeping Spafford's tragedy in mind. Let all of the notes ring for as long as possible, and listen to how a com-bination of ringing open strings and fretted notes, such as those in bars 26 and 29, add a moving quality to this beautiful hymn. And remember, especially when playing the block chords throughout: it's all about the melody.

Tuning: D A D G B D

Nearer, My God, to Thee

"Nearer, My God, to Thee" made it into popular culture through films that depicted it being played as the *Titanic* went down. Although there is much controversy over whether the song was actually played on the *Titanic*, it seems quite likely that it was sung by passengers on another doomed ship—the *SS Valencia*—as she sank in the freezing waters off Vancouver Island in 1906.

I have arranged the piece in two sections: one somber, the other not so much. Although they are basically independent arrangements, I recommend learning the slow version first. In addition to being more accessible, it is also the more beautiful of the two, and the one you may want to play when you find yourself or those around you in need of soothing. If you undertake the faster version, starting with the slower rendition will also get you oriented for some of the very challenging fretting-hand variations that are even more daunting at snappier tempos.

Of course, the fact that this is a serious song doesn't mean you can't have a bit of fun with it. The faster version begins in measure 35; you might call this the "If you're going down, you might as well be dancing" section. The toughest part is the series of lightning-fast notes that appears in measure 67 and again in measure 92. Don't let these fancy bass runs deter you from playing the piece—if you can't get them down, substitute a bass run of your choosing. I strongly recommend practicing this piece slowly with a metronome about a zillion times (or until you can play it smoothly). The payoff is huge!

Tuning: D A D G B D
Slow Version

Fast Version

Love Divine, All Loves Excelling

"Love Divine, All Loves Excelling" just might take the award for longest hymn name. I first heard the song in 1984, when I was putting myself through college, working as a security guard in an old-folks' home. When I heard one of the residents play it on the piano and sing her heart out, I was struck by the song's bombastic quality.

"Love Divine" also gets a prize for the most notes crammed into the shortest space. I play it in the key of D major in DADGAD tuning, using a lot of block chords and moving bass lines. It definitely gives the fretting hand a workout, and it might in fact be the hardest arrangement in this collection.

The good news is that my interpretation can be stream-lined—especially in the bass line—to make it easier to play. For instance, you might just cut out the notes on the *ands* of certain beats, like the open A string on beat 2.5 in bar 1 and the fifth-fret G on beat 4.5 in that same measure.

Whether you play the arrangement as written or with fewer notes, it's best to use a metronome and start slowly, gradually increasing the tempo as you get the fretting-hand moves in your muscle memory. Keep at it until you can run the tune flawlessly—and most important, animatedly—at tempo.

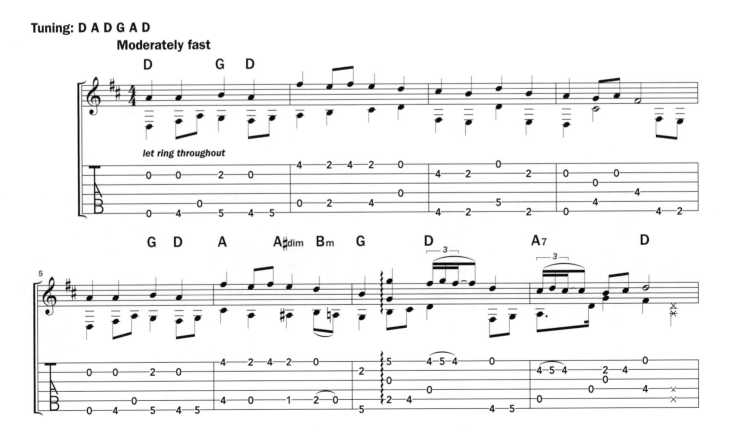

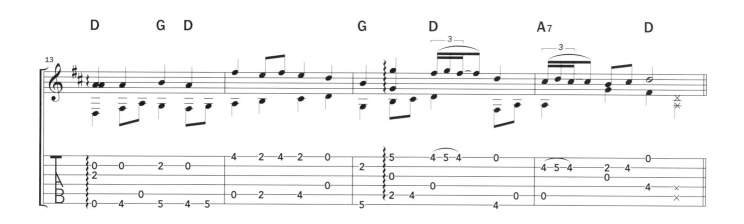

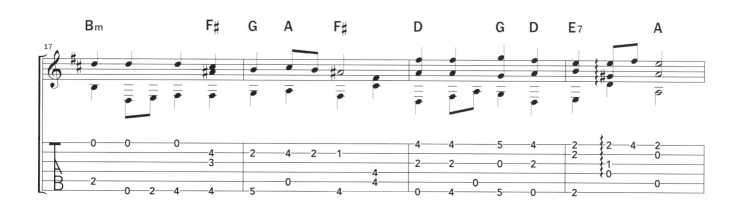

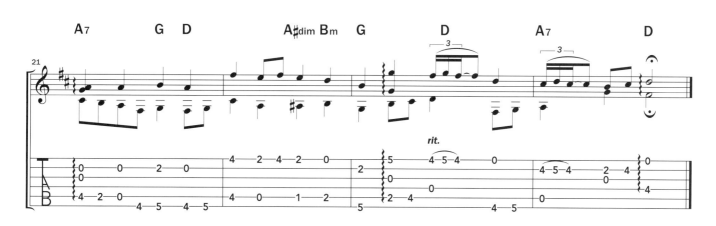

Softly and Tenderly

"Softly and Tenderly" is one of the great old invitation hymns, which I first heard in the Southern Baptist scene that I grew up in. On guitar, I play the piece in Orkney; those who know my music know that I'm a big fan of this tuning. If Orkney is unfamiliar, don't let it scare you, because you'll see how it allows the piece to flow with very little effort.

Orkney tuning is spelled, lowest string to highest, C G D G C D. That's two Cs, two Gs, and Ds, the open strings forming a deep and rich Csus2 chord. To access Orkney from standard tuning, lower string 6 by two steps and strings 5 and 1 by one step each; raise string 2 by a half step.

In my arrangement of "Softly and Tenderly," I use a combination of fretted notes and open strings that cascade together in a beautiful, harp-like way. An added benefit of this approach is that it's easy on the fretting hand, making the piece a great introduction to Orkney and to open tunings in general.

Play the piece gently, in an unrushed way, rendering the melody as sweetly as possible. Where you see the staccato markings (noteheads with dots), cut short the fretted notes by releasing pressure on your fretting fingers. Otherwise, let all the notes ring throughout. Hold down each note/chord shape for as long as possible—keep those notes alive until you can't let them live anymore.

C G D G C D

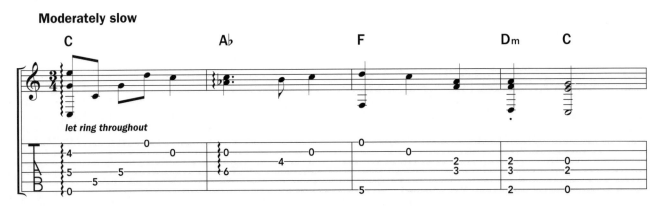

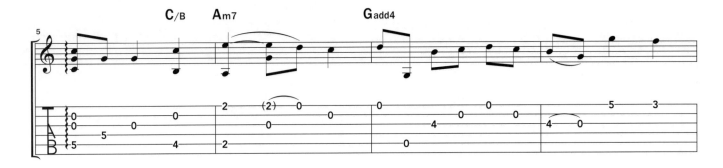

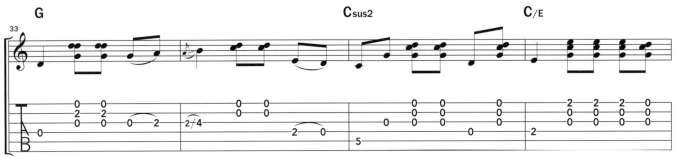

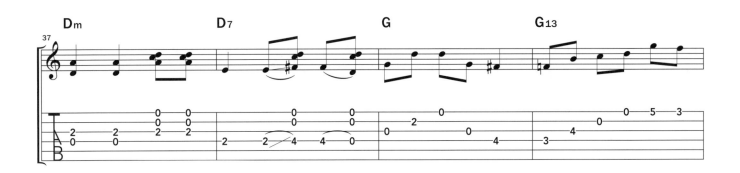

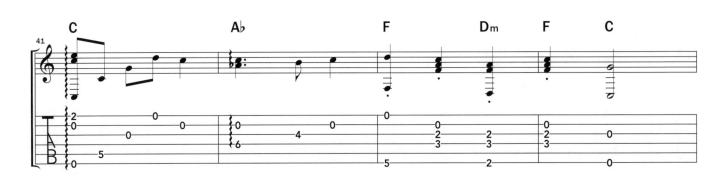

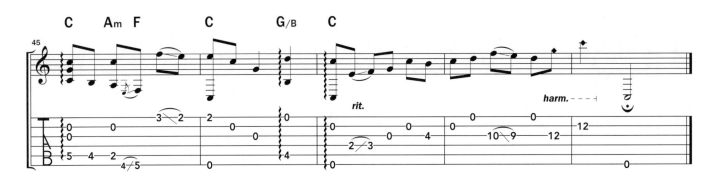

What a Friend We Have in Jesus

"What a Friend We Have in Jesus" is one of the classic standards, and it's most often done in a goody-two-shoes sort of way. But being a fingerstyle guitarist, I claim the right to jazz it up and bluesify it, with an alternating-thumb pattern in dropped-D tuning.

When you play my arrangement of "What a Friend We Have in Jesus"—or really any alternating-thumb piece—I strongly recommend palm-muting the bass notes. (Remember, rest your picking-hand palm on the strings, so that the sound is slightly muffled.) This creates a nice textural contrast while allowing the melody to stand out.

I'd like to point out my use of the "Deep River Blues" E7 chord (which I also play in "Pass Me Not, Oh Gentle Savior" and "Rock of Ages") slid down two frets here for a D7 chord. (See bars 7–8 and elsewhere.) It's just a sweet chord to know

in dropped-D tuning, especially if you have a propensity for country-blues stylings—and if you're reading this book, there's a good chance that you do.

Another thing that this arrangement illustrates is that it's OK to have a moving bass line, chords, and melodies all of a sudden stop and yield to a leaner texture. This happens, for instance, in bar 55. Things don't fall apart when the bass line exits, but rather, the listener's attention is drawn to a cool, bluesy single-note line. In other words, you don't have to keep a multiplicity of parts going at all times, and it keeps a listener engaged when you switch things up like this.

Admittedly, the "Deep River Blues" chord and the bluesy break are much less important than the melody to "What a Friend We Have in Jesus." It's such a widely known song that it's important to play it nice and strong and clean throughout the arrangement.

Tuning: D A D G B E

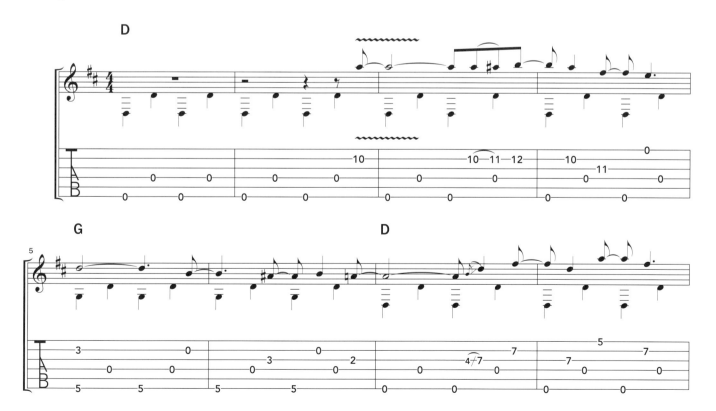

About the Author

Steve Baughman has been performing guitar and banjo around the world for nearly four decades. An innovative instrumentalist known for exploring alternate tunings, Baughman has developed a clawhammer guitar technique and helped make it common practice for fingerstyle guitarists. He has taught at over 70 music camps across the United States and Canada and has toured for 10 years as a duo with the Celtic guitarist Robin Bullock.

Baughman has written a handful of instructional books and appears on multiple CDs, three of which— *Farewell to Orkney*, *Celtic Guitar Summit* (with Bullock), and *Clawhammer Guitar: The Collection* (various artists)—have been featured in *Acoustic Guitar* magazine.

Baughman makes his home in the San Francisco Bay Area where, when he is not performing or teaching, he is a part-time philosophy graduate student and attorney.

For more on the work of Steve Baughman, visit www.celticguitar.com.

GOSPEL SONGS FOR FINGERSTYLE GUITAR

This is one in a series of **Acoustic Guitar Guides** that help you become a better guitarist, a smarter shopper, and a more informed owner and user of guitars and gear.

See the complete collection at **Store.AcousticGuitar.com**.

You'll also find . . .

Get to know the music, musicians, and instruments that matter. For beginning to professional guitarists, teachers, and members of the trade, too.

Information, instruction, and inspiration for every guitar player. Reference, how-to, songbooks, and more.

From lessons and songs to tuners and tees, the Acoustic Guitar store has something for you. Visit **store.acousticguitar.com** today.

The Acoustic Guitar website features stories you won't want to miss—gear reviews, breaking news, performance videos, giveaways, lessons, and more. Visit **AcousticGuitar.com**.